BANNER 17

BOSTON CELTICS RETURN TO GLORY IN A MAGICAL CHAMPIONSHIP SEASON

The Boston Globe

This book is available in quantity at special discounts
for your group or organization. For further information,
contact:
Triumph Books
542 South Dearborn Street, Suite 750
Chicago, Illinois 60605
Phone: (312) 939-3330
Fax: (312) 663-3557

Printed in the United States of America
ISBN: 978-1-60078-180-3

TRIUMPH
BOOKS

BOOK STAFF
EDITORS Janice Page, Gregory H. Lee Jr.
ASSISTANT EDITOR Ron Driscoll
ART DIRECTOR Rena Anderson Sokolow
DESIGNER Jerome Layman Jr.
PHOTO EDITORS Bruce Pomerantz, Jim Wilson
RESEARCHERS Liberty Pilsch, Bruce Pomerantz
IMAGING Frank Bright, Jerome Layman Jr.

PHOTOGRAPHERS
THE BOSTON GLOBE John Blanding, 108, 111
• John Bohn, 59 • Bill Brett, 108 • Yoon S. Byun, 121
• Barry Chin, 1, 5, 7, 13, 18, 19, 24, 31, 36, 37, 38, 39,
42, 43, 44, 45, 76, 77, 83, 86, 91, 97, 117, back cover
• Jim Davis, front cover, 2, 14, 15, 17, 20, 24, 27, 30,
35, 46, 51, 52, 53, 54, 55, 56, 58, 60, 61, 62, 63, 67,
68, 69, 70, 71, 72, 74, 75, 78, 79, 84, 85, 88, 89, 95,
96, 97, 98, 112, 115, 116, 118, 119, 123 • Dan Goshtigian,
107 • Stan Grossfeld, 12, 16, 29, 85, 111, 120, 128
• Tom Herde, 114 • Justine Hunt, 85 • David
Kamerman, 94 • Matthew J. Lee, 90, 113, 122
• Frank O'Brien, 106, 107, 109 • Jack Sheehan, 98
• John Tlumacki, 101, 110.

ADDITIONAL PHOTOS COURTESY OF
AP/Wide World Photos, 11 (Winslow Townson),
22 (Kevork Djansezian), 23 (Mark Avery, Mark J.
Terrill), 24 (Mark J. Terrill), 47 (Gary Malerba), 57
(Mark Duncan), 72 (Gregory Smith), 84 (Plinio
Lepri), 88 (Chuck Burton), 92 (Eric Gay), 96
(Chuck Burton), 100 (Elise Amendola), 104
(Gene Herrick), 104, 105, 108, 125 (Stephan Savoia)
• Elsa/Getty Images, 26 (Stephen Dunn), 40, 85,
90 (Chris Graythen), 124 (Brian Babineau)
• Reuters, 87 (Kevin Kolczynski).

With special thanks to The Boston Globe sports
department, photo and design departments,
Holly Warshaw (IT), and library staff.

Front cover Celtics captain Paul Pierce lets out
a roar on the way to his team's dramatic Game 7
victory over the Cleveland Cavaliers.

Opposite page Pierce hoists the Larry O'Brien
Trophy and Garnett embraces Bill Russell.

Back cover Game 1 of the NBA Finals started with
a bang at Boston's TD Banknorth Garden, but that
was just the beginning of the fireworks.

CONTENTS

6 Introduction by Marc J. Spears

8 **NBA FINALS**
A dream match-up reviving basketball's most storied rivalry gave us new heroes, blowouts, and comebacks worthy of legend.

32 **EASTERN CONFERENCE FINALS**
The mighty Detroit Pistons fell at home in 6, and the Celtics finally proved they were a team that could win it all.

48 **EASTERN CONFERENCE SEMIFINALS**
An epic Game 7 shootout featured 45 points from LeBron James, but Paul Pierce's Celtics were the ones who survived.

64 **EASTERN CONFERENCE QUARTERFINALS**
Give credit to the pesky Atlanta Hawks. No one gave them any love until they hung around for 7 games.

80 **THE SEASON**
It was the greatest turnaround in history: The Celtics, buoyed by a new Big Three, went from worst in their division to first in the NBA.

98 **BACK & FORTH**
Remembering Red, banners 1-16, profiles, team roster, and game-by-game stats and summaries.

June 17, 2008 • BY MARC J. SPEARS/Globe Staff

Somewhere Red Auerbach is smiling. ⊕ After a 22-year wait, the Celtics finally earned a 17th championship banner and they did it in triumphant fashion, at home on the parquet floor that now bears Auerbach's name. ⊕ The longest season by any NBA team began with training camp in Rome, included 82 regular-season games, and ended with a league-record 26 post-season contests. Led by an All-Star trio of Kevin Garnett, Paul Pierce, and Ray Allen — the new Big Three — these Celtics more than lived up to expectations as they claimed the title by going through their franchise's most storied rival, the Los Angeles Lakers. ⊕ Missing in the longawaited celebration, however, was Auerbach, the former Celtics' coach, general manager, president, and patriarch. For the first time in Boston's banner history, the Hall of Famer, who died nearly two years ago, was not part of a Celtics championship. But when all was said and done, the Celtics not only pulled out cigars in honor of Red, they kept his fabled record intact. ⊕ Auerbach and Lakers coach Phil Jackson both have an NBA-record nine championships. Jackson had a chance to surpass Auerbach by beating the Celtics. But the Celtics protected Auerbach's honor by playing the kind of old-school basketball that brought him 16 championship rings. ⊕ As in the days of Bill Russell, Boston played the most stifling defense in the league. And despite their long list of accomplishments, All-Stars, and even championship rings, this veteran group was unified by the same kind of team spirit that characterized Auerbach's squads. Coach Glenn "Doc" Rivers even gave it a name by borrowing the South African word for unity: ubuntu. ⊕ The Celtics' shorts are now much longer than the tight ones Bob Cousy used to wear. Today the team plays in TD Banknorth Garden; the old Boston Garden is a parking lot. The game is faster and much more athletic than it used to be. But the 2007-08 Celtics succeeded by getting back to the style of play that brought them title after title. Soon, that elusive 17th banner will be raised at the new Garden. Then, as now, Red will be smiling.

39

The 131-92 win in Game 6 was the largest margin of victory in an NBA title-clinching win.

26

The Celtics played an NBA-record 26 playoff games, going 16-10 overall and 13-1 at home.

22

Ray Allen hit a record 22 3-pointers in the Finals, including a record-tying 7 in Game 6.

18

The Celtics had a record 18 steals in the clincher, eclipsing Golden State's 17 in 1975.

17

On the 17th day of June 2008 (exactly 22 years after Len Bias was drafted), the Celtics finally captured Banner 17.

Kobe Bryant had drawn comparisons to Michael Jordan, but his star faded in the Finals. In the end, it wasn't about the Big Three, but about all the little things that add up to titles. Oh, and a rally from 24 points down on your opponent's home court, that helps.

Game 1

98-88

LA	21	30	22	15	88
BOS	23	23	31	21	98

THURSDAY, JUNE 5, 2008 • **BOSTON** ⓦ○○○○○○

Game 2

108-102

LA	22	20	19	41	102
BOS	20	34	29	25	108

SUNDAY, JUNE 8, 2008 • **BOSTON** ⓦⓦ○○○○○

Game 3

87-81

BOS	20	17	25	19	81
LA	20	23	17	27	87

TUESDAY, JUNE 10, 2008 • **LOS ANGELES** ⓦⓦⓛ○○○○

Game 4

97-91

BOS	14	26	31	26	97
LA	35	23	15	18	91

THURSDAY, JUNE 12, 2008 • **LOS ANGELES** ⓦⓦⓛⓦ○○○

Game 5

103-98

BOS	22	30	18	28	98
LA	39	16	24	24	103

SUNDAY, JUNE 15, 2008 • **BOSTON** ⓦⓦⓛⓦⓛ○○

Game 6

131-92

LA	20	15	25	32	92
BOS	24	34	31	42	131

TUESDAY, JUNE 17, 2008 • **BOSTON** ⓦⓦⓛⓦⓛⓦ○

LAKERS RIVALRY

They are not your old man's Celtics. No black canvas high-tops. No cigar smoke wafting toward the Garden rafters from the Boston bench. No behind-the-back passes from Cooz, and no Larry Legend smashing his face on the parquet floor. ⊕ But the 2007-08 Boston Celtics are champions of the world, worthy successors to the men your dad always told you about. ⊕ The Celtics returned to glory last night, winning their 17th NBA title – their first banner since 1986 – with a 131-92 Game 6 dismemberment of the soft-shell Lakers at the Causeway Street Gym. ⊕ It felt like a restoration of the natural order of the basketball universe. ⊕ The finale, Boston's record 26th postseason game of 2008, was an homage to the 12-man selflessness, teamwork, and ferocious defense that marked the golden days of Green dominance. Kevin Garnett and Ray Allen led the champs with 26 points apiece while second-year guard Rajon Rondo scored 21 to go with 7 rebounds and 8 assists. ⊕

 Celtics captain and Finals MVP Paul Pierce scored 17 points and had 10 assists, and Boston's bench won the game in a 34-15 second quarter that demoralized the visitors and made the second half more coronation than competition. ⊕ In bygone days when dinosaurs ruled the earth and Bill Russell roamed the paint, the Celtics were the signature franchise in pro ball. Internationally famous, they won 16 championships between 1957 and 1986, including eight straight with Red Auerbach on the bench. ⊕ They disappeared from the local sports landscape in recent seasons, but re-emerged in full championship fury after general manager Danny Ainge acquired Garnett and Ray Allen in the summer of 2007. Boston won 66 games in the regular season and went 13-1 at home during the 68-day postseason tournament. ⊕ Brilliantly coached by Doc Rivers, sculpted with Auerbachian guts and guile by Ainge (who learned it all at the right hand of Red), the Celtics won the title one year after a 24-58 campaign, which included an 18-game losing streak. › PAGE 30

FROM THEIR
FIRST MEETING
IN PRESEASON,
THE CELTICS'
BIG THREE
ALWAYS HAD
THEIR EYES ON
THE PRIZE.

GAME 1

As he lay on the court in the third quarter, his knee throbbing, Paul Pierce thought, "It can't be over like this." After being carried to the locker room, Pierce made a dramatic return. His 11 points after coming back – including two quick 3-pointers – were critical, but the emotional lift he provided was just as important.

GAME 1

Just as he tangled with LeBron James in an earlier round, Paul Pierce often drew Kobe Bryant head-to-head. Bryant struggled in Game 1, hitting just 9 of his 26 shots, although his 24 points led the Lakers. "I had some good looks, they just didn't go down for me," he said.

GAME 2

Pregame warmups were crucial for Kendrick Perkins and Paul Pierce, who were coming off Game 1 injuries. Pierce showed few ill effects, scoring 28 points to lead the way as the Celtics built a huge lead and held on to win. Fans of No. 5, Kevin Garnett, were pleased with his 17-point effort.

GAME 2

Leon Powe provided a tremendous lift off the bench, scoring 21 points in 15 minutes. Powe keyed a 15-2 run to end the third quarter as Boston took a 24-point lead, but in an eerie precursor to the Lakers' Game 4 woes, Boston almost let the lead slip away. Vladimir Radmanovic's steal and breakaway dunk helped LA get within 2 points, but Pierce thwarted the rally.

GAME 3

Doc Rivers exhorts his team as they come to the sidelines in the final minute of Game 3. The Celtics led by 2 points entering the fourth quarter, but were outscored, 27-19, in the final 12 minutes as regular-season MVP Kobe Bryant scored 36 points, including some key baskets down the stretch. After the Celtics took 38 free throws to LA's 10 in Game 2, the Lakers had a 34-22 edge in Game 3. Paul Pierce went 2-for-14 from the field, and Kevin Garnett hit just 6 of 21 shots.

GAME 4

The Lakers were soaring early, as Kobe Bryant, Lamar Odom (7), and Sasha Vujacic jumped on the Celtics for a 35-14 lead after one quarter. The lead crested when Vujacic hit a 3-pointer to make it 45-21. Bryant and Co. were still leading by 20 halfway through the third quarter...

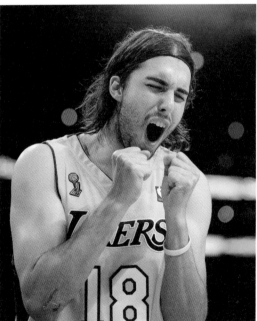

... But the Celtics proceeded to start a rally of historic proportions. P.J. Brown (93) dunked over Bryant to cap a 21-3 run to end the third quarter and cut the lead to 73-71. Eddie House (13 points) and James Posey (18) played major roles, and Ray Allen sealed the victory with a drive past Pau Gasol with 16 seconds to play. Bryant found his way blocked by Pierce and Garnett. "I saw three, four bodies every time I touched the ball," he said.

GAME 5

From left to right, Lamar Odom, Kobe Bryant, Ray Allen, Kevin Garnett, Pau Gasol, and P.J. Brown follow the bouncing ball in Game 5 at the Staples Center. The Lakers roared to another early lead, much to the chagrin of Doc Rivers, who argues with referee Dick Bavetta as Jack Nicholson gleefully butts in. Unlike Game 4, LA did not crumble, despite 38 points from Paul Pierce. Bryant made a key swipe and breakaway dunk in the final minute as the Lakers brought the series back to Boston with a 103-98 victory.

In a common sight in the clinching game, Paul Pierce corrals the loose ball as Kobe Bryant and the Lakers come up empty. The Celtics were credited with a Finals-record 18 steals, and their defense triggered a 26-6 run late in the first half that broke the game open. (Following page) If it wasn't Ray Allen hitting one of his record-tying seven 3-pointers, the defining offensive moment was probably Kevin Garnett's bank-shot 3-point play while being fouled by the Lakers' Lamar Odom late in the first half that stretched the lead to 56-35. Rajon Rondo, who shot 1 for 7 and played just 14 minutes in Game 5, bounced back with 20 points, eight assists, seven rebounds, and six steals in the series clincher.

FROM 10 • The champs struggled in seven-game series against the Hawks and Cavaliers (0-6 on the road) before finding their voice in a six-game set against the formidable Pistons.

"This is unreal," Pierce told the crowd. "I'm just happy that ... everybody, the city of Boston stuck with me throughout all the hard times. I know we didn't have a lot of great years, but you guys stuck with me, and now we bring home a championship to you."

The victory cements Boston's claim as Titletown, USA. Boston is home of the world champion Celtics and the world champion Red Sox. Now if only that slacker team in Foxborough can get with the program.

Boston made only 9 of 24 shots in an erratic first quarter, but led, 24-20, thanks to the hot hand of Garnett. Called out by peers (Ron Artest) and NBA watchers from coast to coast, Garnett scored 10 in the quarter, and paced the Celtics to an early lead despite poor shooting.

The Celtic bench (more kudos for Ainge) took back the night in the second. Posey (11 points, one of five Celtics in double figures) and House hit back-to-back treys from the left corner to put the Celtics up by 9 and force Jackson to call a panic timeout.

It didn't help. The Celtics effectively won the championship with a 15-2 quarter-closing run to make it 58-35 at intermission. The Lakers spit back whopping leads on their home court. The Celtics do not.

The Celtics ran to a 79-48 lead midway through the third while the poet on the Laker bench just stood back and let it all be.

The Vault was a victory Garden in the final 12 minutes. Rivers took out his starters when it was 116-81 with 4:01 left. The lead peaked at 43 when Tony Allen flushed home a reverse dunk to make it 129-86.

Late in the fourth, while some fans lit cigars, Ainge's image appeared on the big board and he refused to even crack a smile. He was a bum at this time a year ago. Now he's a hero on a par with Bill Belichick and Theo Epstein.

Light it up. The Boston Celtics, once synonymous with sports supremacy, are back where they belong. ⊕

The Pistons had been here before – a lot. But the Celtics picked a perfect time to solve their road malaise. Just as they had all season, they let their defense set the tone and silenced the Palace din.

Game 1

88-79

	1	2	3	4	
DET	17	23	17	22	79
BOS	22	19	28	19	88

TUESDAY, MAY 20, 2008 • **BOSTON** W○○○○○○

Game 2

103-97

	1	2	3	4	
DET	18	32	28	25	103
BOS	20	23	26	28	97

THURSDAY, MAY 22, 2008 • **BOSTON** WL○○○○○

Game 3

94-80

	1	2	3	4	
BOS	25	25	23	21	94
DET	17	15	23	25	80

SATURDAY, MAY 24, 2008 • **DETROIT** WLW○○○○

Game 4

94-75

	1	2	3	4	
BOS	17	22	19	17	75
DET	22	21	22	29	94

MONDAY, MAY 26, 2008 • **DETROIT** WLWL○○○

Game 5

106-102

	1	2	3	4	
DET	23	23	25	31	102
BOS	23	29	32	22	106

WEDNESDAY, MAY 28, 2008 • **BOSTON** WLWLW○○

Game 6

89-81

	1	2	3	4	
BOS	24	16	20	29	89
DET	21	16	31	13	81

FRIDAY, MAY 30, 2008 • **DETROIT** WLWLWW○

PISTONS

PROWESS

May 31, 2008 • BY BOB RYAN/Globe Staff

Doubts, there were always doubts. ⊕ Could the guys with the big reps and the big paychecks play together? Was the supporting cast capable of being supportive enough? Could they win on the road? Could they win on the West Coast? A 66-16 record answered all those queries. ⊕ Then came the playoffs. ⊕ There was the road thing. Seven games against the eighth seed? Bad. More road struggles against Cleveland. Two seven-game series in a row. Bad. Were they really championship-worthy? ⊕ Game 3 in Detroit. There was no choice. They had lost Game 2, so they had to win a game here, and they did. But two? Could they win another? Could they close the deal without risking another seventh game? ⊕ There are no more questions. On May 30 in Auburn Hills, Mich., the Celtics closed the deal. They not only won an elimination game in the Eastern Conference finals, they did so with a monster comeback, a fourth-quarter performance that will go down in

R O U N D 3

Celtics history. They won a big playoff game on the road and they won it in a style that the Russells, Cousys, Havliceks, and Birds could be proud of. ⊕ "I could write a long book about my emotions right now," said Paul Pierce, who scored 12 of his 27 points in the fourth quarter as the Celtics won the Eastern Conference championship for the 20th time with an 89-81 victory over the Detroit Pistons. ⊕ Trailing by 10 points (70-60) a minute and a half into the fourth quarter after being hit with a 22-6 Detroit run, the Celtics reached down for that certain something and began acting like a championship team at both ends of the floor. As usual, the average guy will remember the offense, whether it was the bookend baskets by Rajon Rondo on a 28-9 run, the go-ahead, spinning 3-point play by Pierce, or the big buckets by Kevin Garnett, who shook off a 2-for-10 first half to come up very big in the deciding fourth quarter. ⊕ But you can bet the coaches will be rhapsodizing over a Boston defense that held the Pistons to 13 fourth-quarter points. You can bet they'll be › PAGE 43

GAME 1

The Celtics and Ray Allen seized the advantage in Game 1. Kevin Garnett led the way with 26 points, 9 rebounds, and a block of a Richard Hamilton shot. Boston took charge with a 28-17 advantage in the third quarter and went on to post an 88-79 win. Detroit's Chauncey Billups, who strained a hamstring in the previous series against Orlando, went 40 minutes between baskets and had just 9 points and 2 assists.

 GAME 2

The home-court advantage was gone. A 103-97 loss meant the Celtics would need at least one road 'W.' Richard Hamilton scored 25 points to lead the Pistons, and Chauncey Billups (19 points, 7 assists) returned to form. Ray Allen scored 25, his highest total in three months, but Theo Ratliff (42) hounded Paul Pierce, and when Kevin Garnett and Rasheed Wallace embraced at the end, Boston had fallen to 9-1 at home in the postseason.

G A M E 3

In a game of runs, the Celtics rebounded for their first road playoff win, 94-80. Boston scored the first 11 points, and a 12-0 blitz in the third quarter helped them build a 24-point lead and improve to 1-6 on the road in the playoffs. "We didn't come out and play," said Pistons rookie guard Rodney Stuckey (3). James Posey and Rajon Rondo (9), battling Antonio McDyess for the ball (next page) had 12 points each for Boston.

FROM 34 • discussing the play of Kendrick Perkins, Garnett, and, most of all, James Posey, who seemed to be guarding five guys at once, and who had a huge steal in the backcourt from a napping Tayshaun Prince at a point when the Pistons were down only 4 at 83-79.

Pure and simple, the only people in the building who thought the Celtics were going to win this game after a 6-point third-quarter lead (54-48)

turned into a 10-point fourth-quarter deficit (70-60) were them. The last seven minutes of the third quarter were beyond ugly from a Boston viewpoint. Detroit appeared to have gained control of the game. A third consecutive seventh game loomed.

No one had more reason to feel aggrieved than Pierce, who had lost a chance for a third-quarter 4-point play when referee Bennett Salvatore mysteriously called an offensive foul

after Pierce had up-faked Prince.

"You know, I was a little upset at that call," Pierce said. "I didn't let it frustrate me, like probably in the past. I probably would have lost my poise, lost my cool, got a technical."

The fourth quarter started very inauspiciously for the Celtics. First there was a shot-clock violation and then there was an offensive foul on Ray Allen. Richard Hamilton (21 points) hit a jumper, and it was 70-60, Detroit, and The Palace of Auburn Hills banshees were howling.

Rondo got them started with a patented floater that triggered a stunning 10-0 run. Pierce put them ahead to stay with a spinning 3-point play (75-74). And Rondo finished it with a shot he certainly would never even have attempted when the season began. With the Celtics up, 81-76, the 22-year-old point guard took a pass from Posey and calmly swished a right corner jumper. It was Boston's final basket, the one allowing them to breathe.

"I had told him, `You've worked all year on that in-between jumper,'" said Doc Rivers. "Use it."

Each of the stars had a moment. Allen was the man with the early hot hand, scoring 13 of his 17 points in the first half. Garnett came to life in the second half. And Pierce, the man who had gotten them through Game 7 with the Cavaliers, was immense in the fourth quarter. Once again, he acted the way a man wearing that "C" is supposed to act.

"I just wanted to keep my poise, just start thinking about the previous games where the games were close in the fourth quarter and just wanted to get a good shot every time down the floor," he said. "I thought this was the best fourth quarter we played all playoffs long."

Yes, it was, and they really needed it. This is a team stitched together on the fly, a team that is a brief year removed from praying for the first pick in the lottery. They had to earn some honest to goodness battle scars.

"I was just really proud of ourselves for fighting back and keeping our emotions," Rivers said. "I guess if you're going to the Finals, I don't know if you could script a better way than the way we're going."

GAME 4

It was a lost cause as Rajon Rondo (above left) and Paul Pierce dropped the ball, and Kevin Garnett and Ray Allen absorbed the 94-75 loss. The Pistons got 21 points and 16 rebounds from Antonio McDyess, and Boston's Big Three missed their first seven shots and finished a combined 11-for-38 from the field. Detroit reserve Jason Maxiell scored 14 points and made the game-defining play, a block from behind of a Garnett breakaway dunk.

GAME 5

Ray Allen found his shooting touch, burying a key jumper to help thwart a Detroit rally in a 106-102 win. Allen had 29 points and Kevin Garnett (top right) led the way with 33, but Kendrick Perkins provided the biggest lift, an 18-point, 16-rebound effort that helped Boston build a 17-point lead. Perkins (battling for the ball, center, and getting a hug from Garnett) outrebounded the entire Detroit team, 13-11, in the first half.

G A M E 6

Kevin Garnett and the Celtics would not be denied their first trip to the NBA Finals in 21 years, as they outscored Detroit, 29-13, in the fourth quarter to take the series. Veteran Antonio McDyess pondered the Pistons' third straight 6-game loss in the conference finals. James Posey made a late steal and Paul Pierce (27 points) clinched the win with free throws, then Pierce, owner Wyc Grousbeck, and Celtic legend John Havlicek celebrated.

The danger: LeBron James's ability to take over a series. The solution: Paul Pierce, whose 41 points nearly matched James's 45 in Game 7, as the Celtics again prevailed despite their maddening road ineptitude.

Game 1

76-72

CLE	15	22	15	20	72
BOS	25	16	12	23	76

TUESDAY, MAY 6, 2008 • **BOSTON** Ⓦ○○○○○○

Game 2

89-73

CLE	24	12	15	22	73
BOS	17	27	26	19	89

THURSDAY, MAY 8, 2008 • **BOSTON** ⓌⓌ○○○○○

Game 3

108-84

BOS	13	22	28	21	84
CLE	32	20	27	29	108

SATURDAY, MAY 10, 2008 • **CLEVELAND** ⓌⓌⓁ○○○○

Game 4

88-77

BOS	21	22	22	12	77
CLE	23	22	23	20	88

MONDAY, MAY 12, 2008 • **CLEVELAND** ⓌⓌⓁⓁ○○○

Game 5

96-89

CLE	23	23	17	26	89
BOS	18	25	29	24	96

WEDNESDAY, MAY 14, 2008 • **BOSTON** ⓌⓌⓁⓁⓌ○○

Game 6

69-74

BOS	18	15	17	19	69
CLE	18	24	17	15	74

FRIDAY, MAY 16, 2008 • **CLEVELAND** ⓌⓌⓁⓁⓌⓁ

Game 7

97-92

CLE	13	27	28	24	92
BOS	18	32	23	24	97

SUNDAY, MAY 18, 2008 • **BOSTON** ⓌⓌⓁⓁⓌⓁⓌ

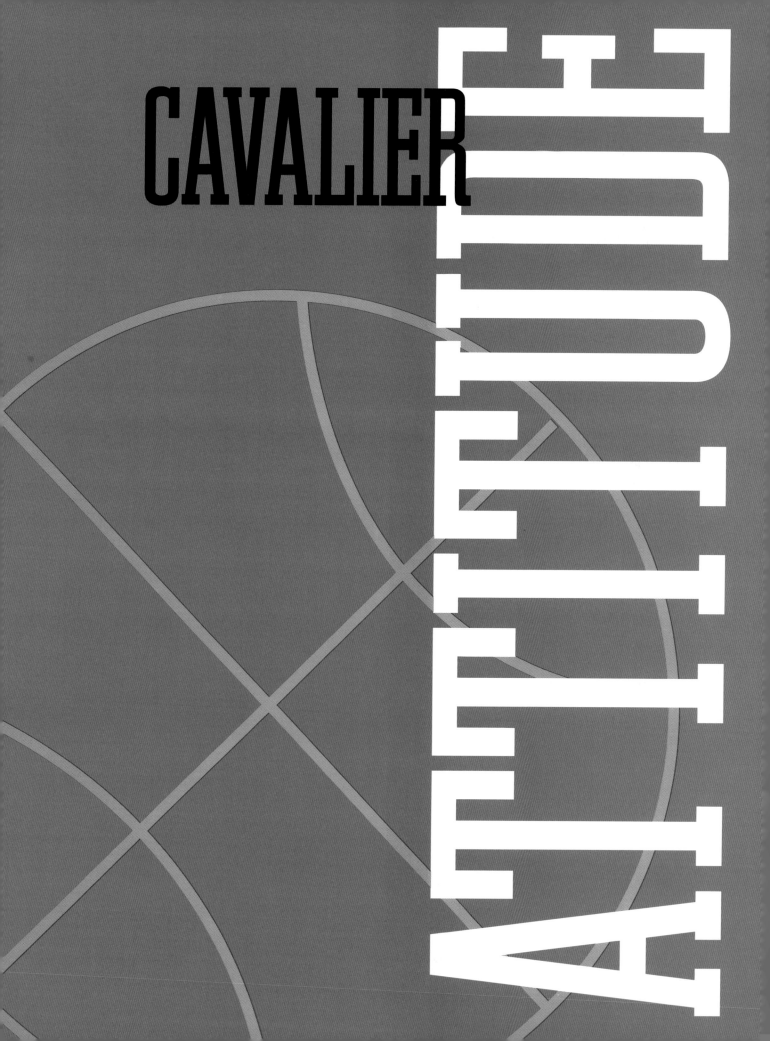

CAVALIER

ALTITUDE

Though the next round probably would be harder, there was good news for the Celtics as they advanced to the Eastern Conference finals against the vaunted Detroit Pistons. They wouldn't have to face LeBron James again. ⊕ James rained 45 points on the heads of the Celtics in an epic Game 7. King James played 46 minutes and 48 seconds, took 29 shots and 19 free throws. He scared the hell out of everyone who bleeds Celtic Green. ⊕ In the pantheon of great performances in losing efforts against the Celtics, LeBron's Sunday Tour De Force was worthy of anything submitted by Bob Pettit, Wilt Chamberlain, Jerry West, or Michael Jordan. And if you're a New England hoop fan over the age of 30, it was impossible to watch Paul Pierce (41 points) and LeBron duel without remembering Larry Bird vs. Dominique Wilkins, circa 1988. "These fans finally have an opportunity to forget a little bit about what Larry Bird and Dominique Wilkins did, and remember what Paul and

ROUND 2

LeBron did," said James, who was 3 years old when Larry and 'Nique matched buckets (34-47 points) in a Game 7 in the Old Garden. ⊕ "It was very exciting to be a part of it, especially in this building," LeBron added after the 97-92 loss. "Like I said, Game 7 in the Garden, it gets no better than this. As a fan of basketball, I know so much about the history ... this will go down in history." ⊕ Bingo. And we don't mean Bingo Smith (Look it up, young 'uns). ⊕ "That's Classic right there," said Kevin Garnett. "I look forward to seeing it on [ESPN] Classic in a couple of days." ⊕ For two weeks Boston basketball fans worried about the Celtics putting themselves in position to let James win the series by himself. Those fears were realized with a couple of minutes left in the final game when the King picked Pierce's pocket and went the length of the floor for a tomahawk stuff. The flush cut Boston's game-long lead to 1 point (89-88) with 2:20 left. It was Game 7, it was close, and LeBron was having his way. ⊕ Fortunately the Celtics had secret weapon P.J. Brown in › PAGE 59

JAMES POSEY (41) GREETS P.J. BROWN AFTER BROWN HIT A KEY JUMP SHOT LATE IN THE CELTICS' GAME 7 VICTORY OVER THE CAVALIERS.

 1

Boston's Kendrick Perkins
holds Sam Cassell after a
hard foul by Cleveland's
Zydrunas Ilgauskas (right)
caused tempers to flare in
the fourth quarter. Cassell
had 13 points off the bench
to help offset 22 from
Ilgauskas as the Celtics
took Game 1, 76-72.

GAME 2

Ray Allen, who was held scoreless in Game 1, gives a small sign of relief after hitting a 3-pointer on the way to a 16-point effort in Game 2. Boston outscored the Cavs, 27-12, in the second quarter thanks to strong bench play from Sam Cassell and Leon Powe on the way to an 89-73 win.

GAME 3

Cleveland's Anderson Varejao and Boston's James Posey exchange words after Posey fouled LeBron James in the first half of Game 3. Sam Cassell can't find a way clear of Cleveland's Joe Smith in the second half of Boston's 108-84 loss. Cassell went 0-for-6 from the field and the Celtics were outscored, 32-13, in the first quarter as the Cavs coasted to victory.

GAME 4

In two of the memorable moments of the series, LeBron James admonishes his mother Gloria after she stood up following a foul on James by Boston's Paul Pierce, then James finishes off a monster dunk over Kevin Garnett. The basket put the Cavs up, 84-75, in Game 4, and they went on to even the series with an 88-77 win. James had 21 points and 13 assists to lead the way,

GAME 5

Paul Pierce howls as his dunk gives the Celtics a double-digit lead in the third quarter of Game 5. A fan tweaks LeBron James over his mother's actions after a Game 4 foul. James scored 35 points, but Boston got 29 points from Pierce, plus 28 points and 16 rebounds from Kevin Garnett, and strong play from Rajon Rondo (20 points, 13 assists) for a 96-89 victory.

FROM 50 · reserve, and Gramps won the game with a big rebound, a clutch jumper, and a baseline stop of LeBron in the final minute.

James's skill and will made this a seven-game series. He did not shoot well from the floor (55 of 155, 35 percent) but he did everything you can do on a basketball court. It was fun to watch. And watch is what most of the Cavaliers ended up doing on offense. It was pretty clear LeBron had no confidence in his supporting cast. In Game 7, the annoying Wally Szczerbiak threw up a doughnut (0 points from the starting shooting guard) and injured sharpshooter Daniel Gibson (shoulder) was missed.

It made you wonder what it's like at practice when Cavaliers coach Mike Brown says, "Let's run the offense." In Game 7, the offense was LeBron and only LeBron. And the Celtics made sure LeBron had to work hard for every one of his 45 points.

My favorite moment of this series came midway though Sunday's third quarter when LeBron and Pierce engaged in a brief, almost collegial exchange during a pause in play. Both smiled after the conversation, then resumed carrying their teams in one of the great duels in Boston sports history.

It reminded me of a chat involving Pete Rose and Carlton Fisk in the 10th inning of Game 6 of the 1975 World Series. The Red Sox and Reds were making history, one great play at a time – perhaps the most important baseball game of the 20th century – when Rose stepped into the batter's box at Fenway Park, turned to Fisk, and said, "This is some kind of game, isn't it?"

It is the whisper of stars. It is rare. And we saw it on May 18 in one of the best duels in the New, or Old, Boston Garden. ⊛

GAME 6

All signs pointed to a Boston loss in Game 6. Wally Szczerbiak (left) celebrates after sinking a 3-pointer over Eddie House (50) to give the Cavs a 72-63 lead late in the game. Delonte West fakes Rajon Rondo into the air, Kevin Garnett nurses a banged-up nose, and Ray Allen leaves the court as the buzzer signals a 74-69 Cleveland win and another Game 7 for Boston.

GAME 7

Paul Pierce and LeBron James found time to smile over their respective performances during a timeout, and Pierce beat James to a crucial loose ball and got a timeout to help the Celtics advance to the Eastern Conference finals. James scored 45 points, but Pierce nearly matched him with 41, and Boston got 10 critical points and 4 rebounds from P.J. Brown to win, 97-92. Kevin Garnett added 13 points and 13 rebounds, and Rajon Rondo had 8 points, 8 rebounds, and 8 assists for Boston.

PIERCE	VS.	JAMES
41	points	45
5	assists	6
4	rebounds	5
0	blocks	0
2	steals	2

This callow crew of Hawks, who went 37-45 during the season, turned into a tough out for Boston, especially in Atlanta, where they fed off their raucous crowd. In the end, the Celtics were safe at home.

Game 1

104-81

ATL	21	19	15	26	81
BOS	29	20	24	31	104

SUNDAY, APRIL 20, 2008 • **BOSTON** W○○○○○○

Game 2

96-77

ATL	20	22	16	19	77
BOS	24	28	24	20	96

WEDNESDAY, APRIL 23, 2008 • **BOSTON** WW○○○○○

Game 3

102-93

BOS	26	30	18	19	93
ATL	32	24	28	18	102

SATURDAY, APRIL 26, 2008 • **ATLANTA** WWL○○○○

Game 4

97-92

BOS	24	24	27	17	92
ATL	29	22	14	32	97

MONDAY, APRIL 28, 2008 • **ATLANTA** WWLL○○○

Game 5

110-85

ATL	19	24	21	21	85
BOS	27	31	23	29	110

WEDNESDAY, APRIL 30, 2008 • **BOSTON** WWLLW○○

Game 6

103-100

BOS	32	18	32	18	100
ATL	20	29	30	24	103

FRIDAY, MAY 2, 2008 • **BOSTON** WWLLWL○

Game 7

99-65

ATL	16	10	17	22	65
BOS	27	17	35	20	99

SUNDAY, MAY 4, 2008 • **BOSTON** WWLLWLW

HAWKS

GAME TIME

HANG TIME

No signs from Paul Pierce. No crop circles sheared into his hair. No "V" for victory, no foam-finger hoisting, and no ambiguous hand signal that could be mimed by the mayor or sanctioned by the commissioner. ⊕ No controversy for the captain. And, best of all, no Game 7 loss in Boston, which would have put the 2007-08 Celtics in the local gulag of all-time chokers. ⊕ Pierce led all scorers with 22 points in the final 99-65 dismemberment of the Atlanta Hawks, which bordered on cruelty. Clearly, the Celtics were intent on avoiding any place in the local Hall of Shame, so they did what they should have done much sooner and finally sent the Hawks south for the summer. ⊕ It was a great day for the Green, but a dreadful afternoon if you were tuning in from Altoona seeking Game 7 drama. This one went right into the pantheon of Game 7 stinkers, alongside the finale of the 1985 World Series (Royals, 11, Cardinals 0) and the Pacers' crushing of the Celtics (97-70)

ROUND 1

just three years ago. ⊕ "I really had no doubt in my mind how we was going to come out tonight," said Pierce. "You kind of saw it from the guys after Game 6 on the plane. There wasn't a lot of talking and we knew that we let a couple games get away in Atlanta and I just knew we was going to take care of business tonight." ⊕ And how. What a beating. The Hawks came out and played the sorry style that yielded a 12-33 road record this year. They hit only three of their first 15 shots and six of 23 in the first quarter, which ended with the Celtics leading, 27-16. ⊕ It got worse for Atlanta. These Hawks would beat the Celtics in the Penn Relays every time, but they weren't going to win a Game 7 in the Garden. Especially not with a point guard who willed himself invisible, Wade Boggs-style, in every Garden game (Mike Bibby had 2 points and 2 assists in 25 minutes of the finale). The only question that remains is how in the name of Pervis Ellison did Atlanta beat the Celtics three times in the series? ⊕ A lot of Green people carried pressure into Game 7. › PAGE 71

KEVIN GARNETT
EXULTS AS LEON
POWE'S BASKET
GIVES THE CELTICS
A 36-POINT LEAD
IN GAME 7, ON
THE WAY TO A
99-65 VICTORY.

GAME 1

The starters (Kendrick Perkins, Rajon Rondo, and Kevin Garnett) clowned on the bench as the reserves completed a 104-81 Game 1 rout of the Hawks. Leon Powe, who scored 10 points and grabbed 4 rebounds in 24 minutes, got a lift from Sam Cassell and Garnett after getting fouled on a dunk in the second half.

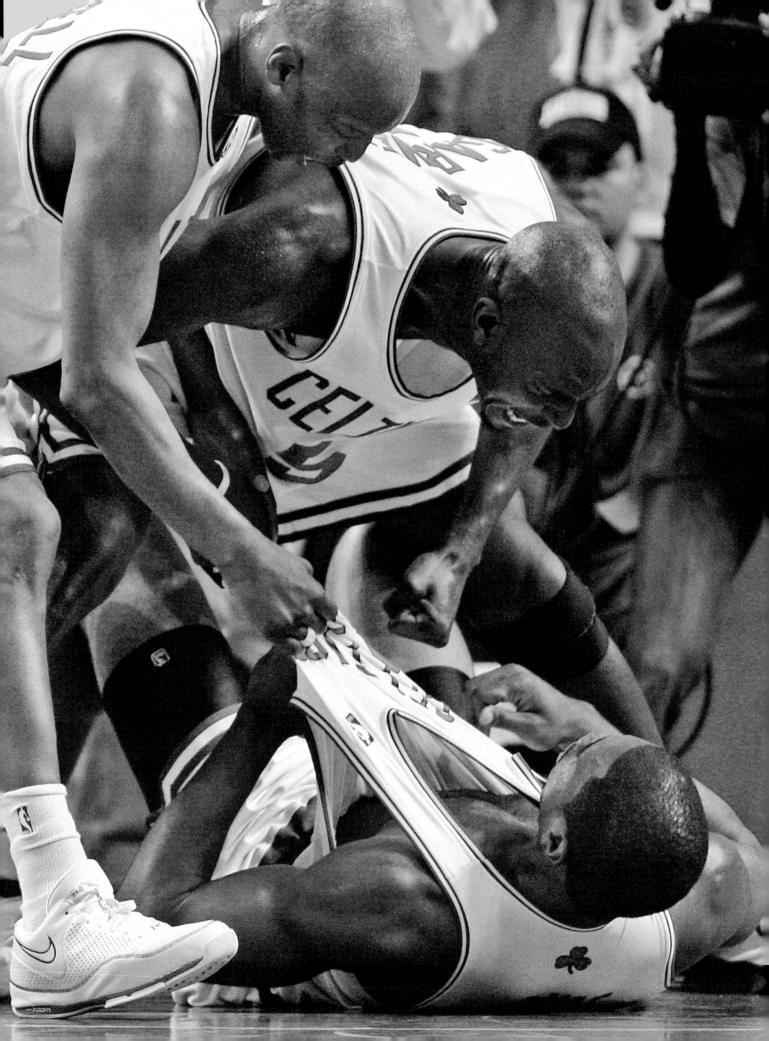

GAME 2

Atlanta coach Mike Woodson is glum as Rajon Rondo runs the Boston offense in Game 2. Rondo had 12 points, 6 rebounds, and 4 steals in a 96-77 win. Rondo had a combined 17 assists and one turnover in his first two career playoff games. Atlanta point guard Mike Bibby (10), who chided the Celtics' "fair-weather fans" before the series, shot 4-for-17 from the field in Games 1 and 2.

FROM 66 • Coach Doc Rivers was carving out a legacy as the hardwood's Marty Schottenheimer and Kevin Garnett was on the spot for not taking the big shots at the end of Game 6. Ray Allen was taking heat for a horrible heave at the end of Game 6, but most of the weight was on the back of the captain.

Pierce's series shot totals were down. He didn't go to the basket and draw fouls in his usual manner. He was fined $25,000 for flashing a "menacing gesture" late in Game 3. He missed an off-balance layup at the end of Game 4. Before Game 5, he issued a statement apologizing for the Game 3 demonstration. He also said he was done talking for the rest of the series. In Game 6, he fouled out with just less than five minutes left (on a horrible call) and drew a technical for tossing his headband in disgust.

So there was a lot of frustration and anxiety entering Game 7, and the Celtics played with appropriate urgency. They never let up. With the score 68-34, Garnett, Allen, and Rajon Rondo all dived on the parquet to save a loose ball. The Boston bench was still standing and cheering when it was 73-37.

"I was telling everybody I was so happy that the game was at 1 o'clock," said Pierce. "Because there was no way I could have sat at home all day."

What about his uncharacteristic silence from Tuesday to Sunday?

"[That was] me and the stuff that was going on with myself," he explained. "I just didn't want to be a distraction to what we was trying to accomplish."

Sounds like a little silent fury, which is a good thing when the Celtics can apply it to their opponent.

The seven-game set proved only that the Celtics are better than the Hawks, which we already knew. The rest of the first-round series is best forgotten. In the end, the victory came with more relief than resolution. ⊕

GAME 3

The opposing No. 5's were going in different directions after Josh Smith led Atlanta to its first playoff victory in nine years. Although Kevin Garnett had 32 points for Boston, Smith had 27 and dunked five times to energize the Hawks and their fans. Paul Pierce, trying to shovel a pass to Rajon Rondo, hit just 5 of 13 shots, and the faces of Kendrick Perkins, Rondo, and Eddie House reflect the 102-93 Atlanta win.

GAME 4

Kevin Garnett and Atlanta's Zaza Pachulia had to be separated in the second quarter of Game 4, leading to technical fouls. "I don't take anything from anybody," said Pachulia after he and the Hawks took the game, 97-92. Atlanta stunned the Celtics behind Joe Johnson, who had 35 points, 20 of them in the fourth quarter. The upstart Hawks went 37-45 during the season, 29 fewer wins than the top-seeded Celtics. "We've got to find ourselves real quick," Boston's Sam Cassell said.

GAME 5

Order was restored, sort of, as the Celtics returned home and posted a 110-85 victory. The Big Three – Pierce (22), Garnett (20) and Allen (19) – led a balanced attack, and Boston's bench outscored Atlanta's, 35-14, helped along by a pair of 3-pointers from James Posey (41). The reserves, behind Sam Cassell (13) and Leon Powe (10), gave Boston a big lift in the second quarter.

The Hawks forced an unlikely Game 7 by posting a 103-100 victory, the sixth straight win by the home team in the series. Joe Johnson hit a 3-pointer with 1:07 to play and a hotly disputed call left Paul Pierce frustrated and fouled him out of the game, powerless to help the Celtics avoid the return trip to Boston. Kendrick Perkins, dunking in the first half, had 14 points for Boston, hitting all of his field-goal tries (5) and free throws (4).

GAME 7

The Celtics ended the suspense quickly, throttling the Hawks into shooting just 29 percent from the field and gradually building a lead that reached 79-43 after three quarters. Atlanta's frustration reached a peak when Marvin Williams tackled Rajon Rondo on a third-quarter breakaway; Williams was ejected from the game. Kevin Garnett, who had 18 points, 11 rebounds, and 3 assists in 27 minutes, was able to watch the Boston reserves finish the game. The Celtics won the four games in Boston by an average of 25 points.

The pieces of the puzzle were glittery and impressive. But no one expected them to fit together so seamlessly from Day 1. A 29-3 start fueled by Kevin Garnett's infectious intensity led to the biggest one-season turnaround in NBA history.

Nov.
13-2
The Celtics open the season 8-0 at home, including a 104-59 win over the Knicks. Their two losses are by 2 (Orlando) and in OT (Cleveland).

Dec.
13-1
They finally lose at home, by 2 to Detroit, but they end the month with 4 straight West Coast wins, including 110-91 over the Lakers.

Jan.
10-5
They hit a rough patch, losing 3 out of 4 to Wizards (twice) and Bobcats, but finish month with a win over Dallas as Kevin Garnett (abdominal strain) sits out.

Feb.
9-4
Celtics go 7-2 in Garnett's absence, then lose the first three games on his return. That first defeat, at Denver, is Boston's first after 16 wins over Western Conference foes.

March
13-3
Ten straight wins bridging February and March is Boston's longest streak of season. They end month with 88-62 win over Heat, in which they hold Miami to an NBA record-low 17 field goals.

April
8-1
Strong finish gives Boston 66 wins, its third-most ever behind 1972-73 (68-14) and 1985-86 (67-15). They end season 25-5 vs. the West, and 35-6 at home.

2006-2007

ATLANTIC	W	L	PCT	GB
Toronto	47	35	.573	-
New Jersey	41	41	.500	6
Philadelphia	35	47	.427	12
New York	33	49	.402	14
Boston	24	58	.293	23

2007-2008

ATLANTIC	W	L	PCT	GB
Boston	66	16	.805	-
Toronto	41	41	.500	25
Philadelphia	40	42	.488	26
New Jersey	33	49	.402	32
New York	24	58	.293	43

For each fan, it was an individual epiphany. ⊕ Just when did hope evolve into expectation for the 2007-08 Celtics? Exactly when did the idea that the Celtics could win the 2008 NBA championship change to the idea that the Celtics should win the NBA championship? ⊕ Was it the 117-97 victory over Phoenix on March 26? ⊕ Was it the three-game Texas conquest of March 17-18-20? ⊕ Was it the 92-85 triumph over the Detroit Pistons at the Palace of Auburn Hills on Jan. 5? ⊕ Was it the four-game West Coast sweep of Dec. 26-27-29-30? ⊕ Or was it the 103-83 destruction of the Washington Wizards on Opening Night, when everyone could see that the Big Three had clearly adopted an All-For-One and One-For-All attitude at both ends of the floor? ⊕ From that riveting start back on Nov. 2, the Celtics were the most relentlessly great team in the league. En route to the league's best record, they reached such checkpoints as 8-0, 29-3, 41-9, and, finally, 66-16, the third-best mark in the storied history of the franchise.

They lost three straight only once (at Denver, at Golden State, and at Phoenix) and that was when Kevin Garnett was working himself back into shape following a debilitating abdominal injury. ⊕ They led the league in lowest opponents' field goal percentage and were just edged out by Detroit in fewest points allowed per game (90.07 to 90.29). They led the league in average victory margin (10.3 ppg) and they won 68 percent (45) of their games by 10 points or more. ⊕ The offense was never an issue. Garnett, Paul Pierce, and Ray Allen fit together seamlessly. The preseason X factor was the maturation process of second-year point guard Rajon Rondo. But the great revelation this year took place when the Celtics did not have the ball. They started out with a defensive mind-set and they never deviated from the plan. ⊕ "That was our challenge, every day," says Garnett. "To be the best defensive team we can be." ⊕ They created a 5 1/2-month buzz for the New England basketball cognoscenti. The Celtics again became a team that's supposed to win. ⊕

IN HIS 10TH
SEASON,
CAPTAIN PAUL
PIERCE COULD
FINALLY SAY
THAT SOMEONE
HAD HIS BACK.

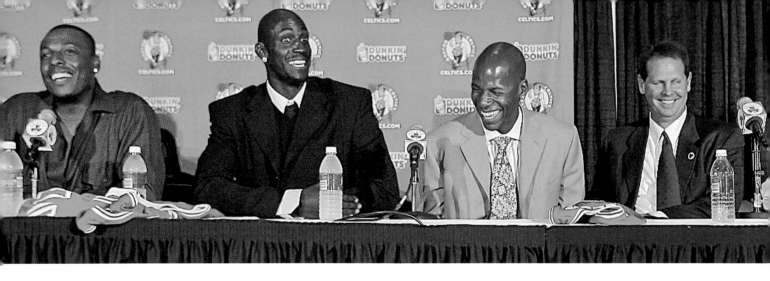

ADVANTAGE, PIERCE
10/6/07

Paul Pierce decides to do as the Romans do, mugging for the camera with some costumed centurions during the Celtics' preseason trip to Europe. The Celtics played games in Rome and London as part of NBA Live Europe, and later cited the opportunity to spend so much time together as a key to their quick start to the regular season

WINNING SMILES 7/31/07

The chemistry was evident from the start when Kevin Garnett (second left) was introduced as a Celtic with (from left) captain Paul Pierce, fellow newcomer Ray Allen, dealmaker Danny Ainge and coach Doc Rivers. Garnett was acquired from the Minnesota Timberwolves for five players and two draft picks, a month after the Celtics traded for Allen on NBA draft night.

DOMINANT DEBUT 11/2/07

Kevin Garnett (5) scored 22 points and snagged 20 rebounds in his first regular-season game as a Celtic, along with 5 assists, 3 steals, and 3 blocks. Ray Allen (with Rajon Rondo and Doc Rivers) had 17, and Paul Pierce led the way with 28 in a 103-83 victory over the Washington Wizards.

WORKING OVERTIME 11/4/07

In the second game of the season, Ray Allen made the winning 3-pointer with less than 3 seconds to go in overtime, and finished with 33 points in a 98-95 victory over the Toronto Raptors. Allen also passed the 17,000-point milestone for his career. Kevin Garnett added 23 points, 10 of them in OT.

Lucky, the Celtics' mascot, performs his nightly acrobatic dunk shot.

EIGHT STRAIGHT 11/16/07

James Posey, who scored 13 points and had 5 rebounds against his former team, celebrates the Celtics' 92-91 win over the Miami Heat. Boston's 8-0 start to the season was its best since the 1972-73 team of John Havlicek, Dave Cowens, and Jo Jo White went 10-0.

MAGIC ENDS 11/18/07

Paul Pierce grimaces as the Celtics go down to their first defeat, 104-102 to the host Orlando Magic. Boston nearly rallied froma 17-point halftime deficit as Pierce led the way with 28 points.

ELEVENTH HOUR 11/24/07

Charlotte Bobcats' guard Raymond Felton won't stand for it after Ray Allen's 3-pointer at the buzzer beat the Bobcats, 96-95, and gave the Celtics an 11-1 record. Allen was 0-for-5 on 3-pointers before hitting the winner, which was set up by a pass deflection from Eddie House.

JAW-DROPPING 11/29/07

Kevin Garnett reacts to the Boston bench players' dominance of the New York Knicks, as the Celtics rolled to a 104-59 win, their largest margin of victory since 1970. Garnett played just 22 minutes in the rout.

MATCH THIS 12/27/07

The Celtics equal their win total for the entire 2006-07 season (24-58) with a victory over the SuperSonics in Seattle, improving to 24-3. They would go on to lose just 16 times all season — they lost their 16th game the previous season on Dec. 26, when they lost at Denver to fall to 10-16.

A young fan appears a bit top-heavy as he awaits the start of a game at TD Banknorth Garden. The team's rejuvenation enabled the Celtics to sell out all 41 home games this season compared to nine sellouts in 2006-07, and their success carried over away from Boston. They were the No. 1 team in the NBA in road attendance, drawing an average of 19,042 fans.

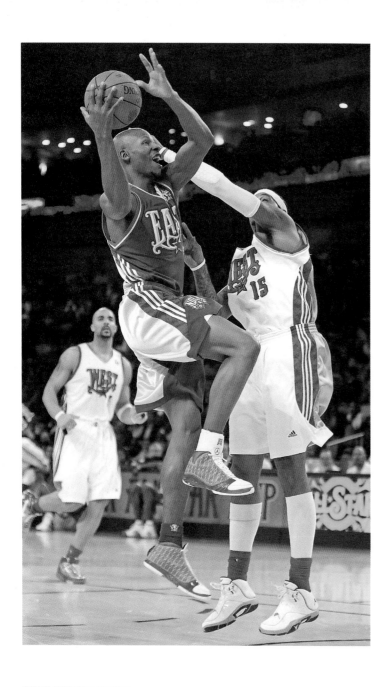

ALL CYLINDERS 3/5/08

Kendrick Perkins slams the ball through for two of his 10 points to go along with 20 rebounds in the Celtics' 90-78 win over the Detroit Pistons. The victory gave the Celtics a 4-game lead over Detroit for the league's best record and also gave Boston the season series, 2-1.

STAR TURN 2/17/08

Ray Allen almost didn't play in the All-Star Game, being named as a replacement for injured Washington guard Caron Butler. But Allen made the most of the chance, scoring a game-high 28 points off the bench to help the Eastern Conference stars defeat the West, 134-128, in New Orleans. Paul Pierce (10 points) and Kevin Garnett (injured) also made the team, and Doc Rivers got the win in his first All-Star coaching gig.

MARCH MILESTONES
3/10/08
The Celtics defeat the 76ers in Philadelphia for their 50th game of the season, reaching that plateau for the first time since 1991-92. They would clinch the Atlantic Division title four days later, despite a loss to the Utah Jazz.

NOTHING DOING 3/14/08
Doc Rivers attempts to shake up his team, which fell behind the Utah Jazz by 10 points early in the game and never recovered in a 110-92 defeat. Deron Williams had 32 points and eight assists to lead the Jazz, who snapped a 10-game Boston winning streak. The Celtics fell to 51-13.

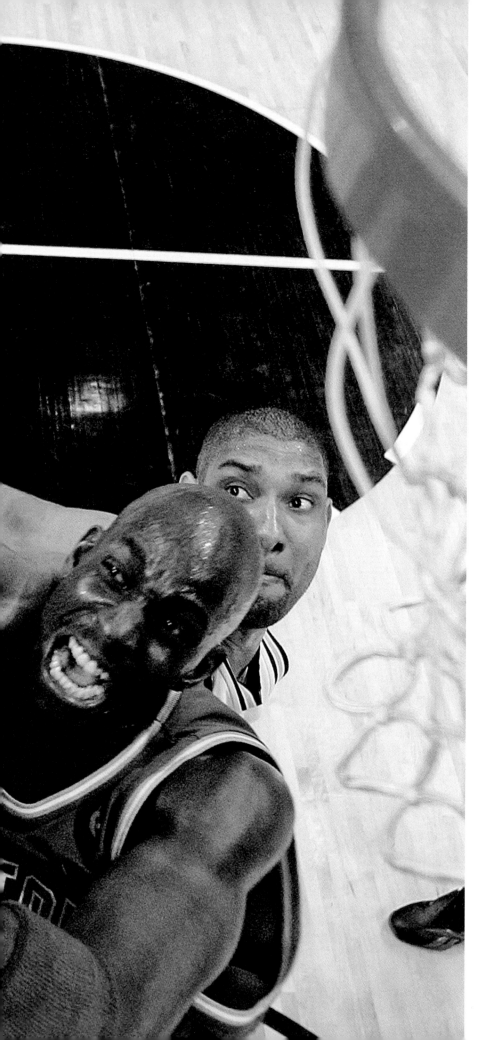

TEXAS TOAST 3/17-20/08

Kevin Garnett battles San Antonio's Tim Duncan for the ball during the Celtics' historic three-game sweep of the NBA's "Texas triangle." Boston beat the Spurs (93-91), the Rockets (94-74), and the Mavericks (94-90) to become the first team since the 2001-02 Sacramento Kings to go 3-0 in a Texas trip. They also ended the Rockets' 22-game win streak, the second-longest in NBA history.

Rajon Rondo drives against
New Orleans point guard
Chris Paul in the Celtics'
112-92 victory over the
Hornets, which gave
them 57 wins to match
their victory total for the
previous two seasons
combined. Rondo hit 8
of 10 shots and scored 17
points to help offset 22
points from Paul.

TAKE A BREAK 4/2/08

Glen Davis spells Kevin
Garnett late in the Celtics'
92-77 home victory over
Indiana. The win was the
60th of the season, giving
Boston its first 60-win
record since 1985-86. The
Celtics have won 60 games
in a season 11 times, the
most in NBA history.

TAKING IT HOME 4/5/08

Tony Allen beats
Charlotte's Jermareo
Davidson to a loose ball in
the Celtics' 101-78 victory.
Allen contributed 12 points
in the win, which clinched
home-court advantage
throughout the playoffs for
the Celtics.

TEAM EFFORT

When the Celtics have wrapped up a victory at home, it's "Gino time," as a 1970s era dance video plays to the delight of fans and players alike. The wins came early and often in 2007-08, thanks in part to the team's embrace of "ubuntu," an African phrase meaning unity. When Kevin Garnett won the league's Defensive Player of the Year, he invited his teammates to share the honor with him. They did.

The original Boston Garden closed in 1995 when a new arena, built adjacent to the site, was opened as the FleetCenter. Renamed TD Banknorth Garden in 2004, the building may have yet another sign change in its future. Doesn't matter. These days, corporate names can come and go faster than Rajon Rondo traverses the parquet. But in Boston, professional basketball is deeply rooted, ever green, and always played in "The Gahden."

BOSTON GARDEN		TD BANKNORTH GARDEN
November 17, 1928	OPENED	September 30, 1995
$4 million	COST	$160 million
11 months	CONSTRUCTION TIME	2 years, 5 months
15,509	MAXIMUM CAPACITY	19,600
14,890	BASKETBALL SEATING	18,854
14,448	HOCKEY SEATING	17,565
0	ESCALATORS	13
1	ELEVATORS	7
36	LUXURY BOXES	104
Non-video	SCOREBOARD	JumboTron
10	BATHROOMS	34
Boxing	FIRST EVENT	Hoisting the banners
No	AIR CONDITIONING	Yes
Parquet	THE FLOOR	Parquet
191x83 feet	RINK SIZE	200x85 feet
Many	OBSTRUCTED VIEWS	None

*Source: TD Banknorth Garden

BACK & FORTH

RED

The Celtics opened their 2007-2008 season on the "Red Auerbach Parquet."

They dedicated the floor at TD Banknorth Garden to the late team patriarch before their season opener on Nov. 2 against the Washington Wizards. The floor now includes Auerbach's signature, which was unveiled by Paul Pierce, Bob Cousy, and Auerbach's daughter, Randy, during a ceremony attended by several Celtics greats.

"The whole Celtics pride thing started with Red Auerbach," Pierce said at the time of the dedication. "Just from him taking me aside from Day 1 here and talking to me means a lot not only in my career but in Celtics history. He's what Celtics pride is all about."

For more than half a century, Arnold "Red" Auerbach was the combative, competitive, and occasionally abrasive personification of pro basketball's greatest dynasty. The Celtics won an NBA-record 16 titles during his 57 years as coach, general manager, and president.

Auerbach was inducted into the Basketball Hall of Fame in 1969 and, 11 years later, was recognized as the greatest coach in NBA history by the Professional Basketball Writers Association of America. His coaching achievement is recognized annually with the awarding of the Red Auerbach Trophy to the league's Coach of the Year.

But Auerbach's genius extended well beyond his coaching. He moved into the Celtics' front office starting in 1966, and by then already had shown his ability to judge talent with the acquisitions of future Hall of Famers such as Bill Russell, John Havlicek, and Sam Jones. Later, as the team's general manager, he would engineer deals for Larry Bird, Kevin McHale, Robert Parish, and Dave Cowens — all of whom also are in the Hall.

He was also a social force in the NBA, drafting the league's first African-American player in 1950 in Chuck Cooper, hiring the first African-American head coach in pro sports in 1966 in Russell, and having five African-Americans as the Celtics' starting lineup in 1964, an NBA first.

In 1980 Auerbach was inducted a second time into the Hall of Fame in recognition of his contributions to the game. He died at 89 years old on Oct. 28, 2006.

"I never thought he'd die," author John Feinstein, who collaborated with Auerbach on "Let Me Tell You a Story: A Lifetime in the Game," told the Associated Press. "He was a unique personality, a combination of toughness and great, great caring about people. He cared about people much more than it showed in his public face, and that's why people cared about him."

Coach Doc Rivers considered Auerbach a close friend he could always solicit for advice.

"Any time you are part of anything that's Red Auerbach, it's special," Rivers said. "Without him, none of us as far as the Celtics and the tradition — even if we had this team that we have coming into this year with all the promise — without Red's contribution in the past, the excitement wouldn't be here."

Asked if he felt sad that Auerbach can't see the reconfigured Celtics, who now include Kevin Garnett and Ray Allen, Pierce said, "He's always going to be here. That's the thing you fail to realize. Red Auerbach will always be with us."

• MARC J.SPEARS & PETER MAY/*Globe Staff*

AUERBACH

"Without Red's contribution in the past, the excitement wouldn't be here."

As 1999 turned to 2000, Sports Illustrated declared the 20 top sports dynasties of the 20th century. At the top stood Celtic center Bill Russell, saluted by SI as "the greatest team player on the greatest team ever." The Green reeled off 11 NBA titles in 13 seasons from 1957 through 1969, and added 2 more in the 1970s (the John

Havlicek era) and 3 in the 1980s (Larry Bird's reign). Yet when people vote for the best single season in NBA history, the 1966-67 Philadelphia 76ers often top the list. Why? Because Wilt Chamberlain and Co. went 68-13 (then the best record ever) and ended the Celtics' run of eight straight titles. Please.

1957 • Red Auerbach came aboard in 1950, as did Bob Cousy. But it wasn't until Russell joined the club that the titles started. Boston used the play of regular-season MVP Cousy and top rebounder Russell to take a thrilling series in seven games over the St. Louis Hawks. The victory was highlighted by a pair of 125-123 double-overtime games — Boston lost the first (Game 1) and won the second (Game 7) for title No. 1.

1959 • Russell hurt his ankle in the 1958 Finals as the Hawks won in six games (winning the four games by an average of two points), but Boston began its record eight-title run the next year. The Jones boys (Sam and K.C.) joined the band, and after surviving a seven-game Eastern finals with the veteran Syracuse Nationals, the Celtics swept the Lakers (then in Minneapolis) for title No. 2.

1960 • Wilt Chamberlain joined the NBA, but his Philadelphia Warriors finished second to the Celtics (59-16) during the season and lost to Boston in a six-game Eastern finals. The Celtics' balanced starting lineup of Tom Heinsohn, Cousy, Bill Sharman, Russell, and Frank Ramsey all averaged at least 15 points a game, and Boston prevailed in a seven-game Finals over St. Louis. Russell grabbed 35 rebounds in an easy 122-103 Game 7 victory.

1961 • The Celtics defeated the St. Louis Hawks for the third time in the Finals after a near carbon-copy of their previous regular season. Boston won 57 games

1959

Tom Heinsohn (15) gives Red Auerbach's ear a tweak after title No. 2.

1963 Bob Cousy, the durable "Houdini of the Hardwood."

1963

Cousy, 34, and Bill Russell after their fifth straight – and final – title together.

Heinsohn puts up a hook shot over the Lakers' Ray Felix in Boston's Game 7 overtime win.

without a player in the league's top 10 in scoring (although this time six players averaged at least 15 points a game). They defeated Syracuse and St. Louis in five games apiece to wrap up their third consecutive crown.

1962 • After a league-best 60-20 record, Boston eked out a seven-game Eastern finals victory over Wilt's Warriors. Both teams won all their home games, and Sam Jones' shot with 2 seconds to play won the series, 109-107. In the Finals, the Celtics rallied from a 3-2 deficit to defeat LA, with the final victory coming in OT. In his career, Russell played in 10 Game 7s and one deciding Game 5 — his record in those pressure contests was 11-0.

1963 • Bill Russell welcomed rookie John Havlicek to the lineup, and the Celtics spread out the scoring, with seven players averaging in double figures. Meanwhile, Wilt Chamberlain was scoring nearly 45 points per game, but his San Francisco Warriors won 27 fewer games than Boston. The Celtics defeated Oscar Robertson and the Cincinnati Royals in seven games in the Eastern finals, then dispatched the Lakers in six games for their fifth straight crown.

1964 • Ho hum: Bob Cousy retired at 34 after the '63 title, but Boston posted 59 wins in the first season without him. Havlicek led the offense with 20 points a game — off the bench. The Celtics cruised to a pair of five-game series

1968 Bill, Red, Hondo.

wins in the playoffs. Cincinnati (with Jerry Lucas joining Robertson) fell in the Eastern finals, the Warriors and Wilt in the Finals. Russell later called this squad the best he played for.

1965 • For the ninth straight year, the Celtics finished with the NBA's best record. They went 62-18 (their best mark in the title run), and Russell won his fifth and last league MVP. They got a scare from Philadelphia and Chamberlain in the Eastern finals before "Havlicek stole the ball" and preserved a one-point win in Game 7. They defeated the Lakers, playing without star Elgin Baylor, in five games for their seventh straight title.

1966 • The remarkable run was nearing its end: Heinsohn had retired and Auerbach announced that it would be his final season as coach. The 76ers edged Boston by one game in the standings, meaning the Celtics would need to win three series for the title. They edged the Royals, 3 games to 2; blitzed Philly, 4 to 1; then slipped by the Lakers in 7 games. Russell averaged 19 points, 25 rebounds, and 5 assists in the playoffs.

1968 • The 76ers ended the streak in 1967, but a "mini-run" would ensue. Russell was the NBA's first black coach, and he was also still the center

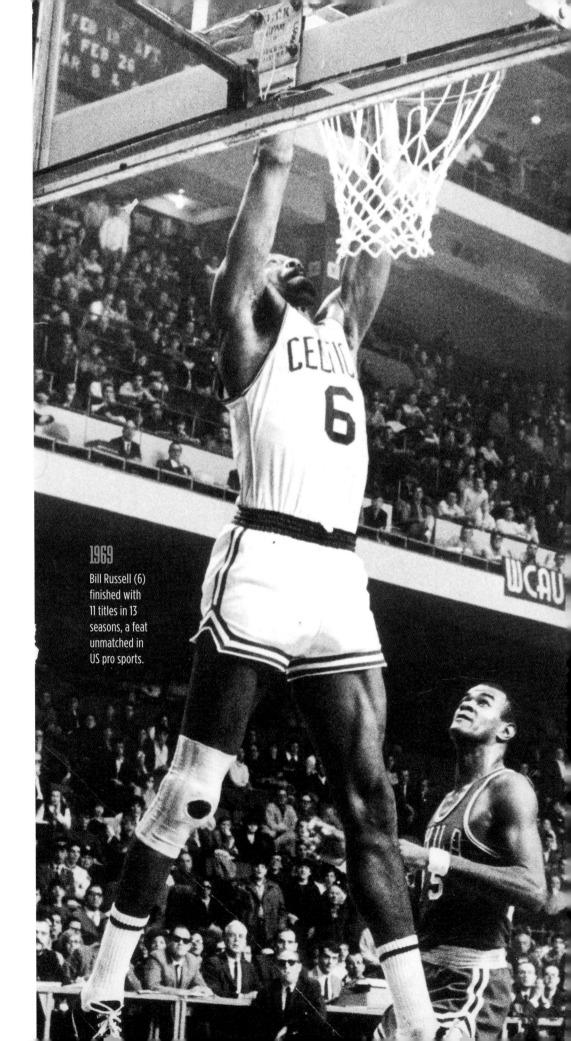

1969

Bill Russell (6) finished with 11 titles in 13 seasons, a feat unmatched in US pro sports.

1969

Sam Jones's basket at the buzzer in Game 4 of the Finals helped the Celtics get the best of Wilt Chamberlain (13) again.

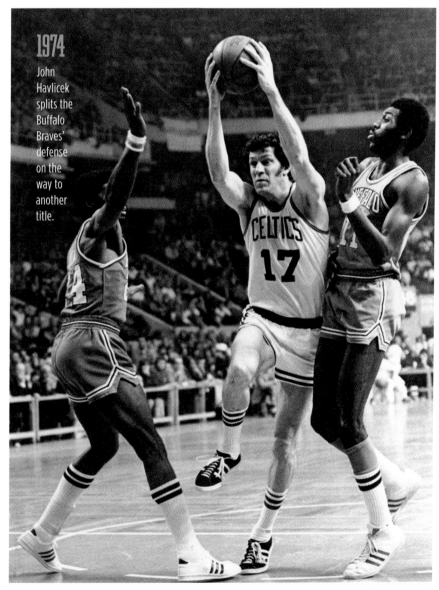

1974

John Havlicek splits the Buffalo Braves' defense on the way to another title.

of the team. The Celtics finished 8 games behind Philly for the season, and trailed them 3 to 1 in the playoffs. Boston rallied to win the final three games by 18, 8, and 4 points, then topped LA in a six-game Finals to regain the trophy.

1969 • Last stand for a dynasty: the Forum in LA, with balloons hung from the rafters to celebrate the favored Lakers' expected Game 7 win. It never happened. The aging Celtics had finished fourth in the East, then beat the Sixers and Knicks to reach the Finals vs. LA, which now had West, Baylor, and Chamberlain. But Boston held on for a 98-96 victory and its 11th title in 13 seasons, a feat unmatched in sports.

1974 • A five-year drought, long by franchise standards at the time, ended with this Havlicek-led squad. "Hondo" had helped bring down Wilt the Stilt, and now he was aiming to ground Milwaukee's Kareem Abdul-Jabbar and his sky hook in the Finals, after ousting Buffalo and New York in the Eastern playoffs. The Celtics lost a dramatic double-overtime Game 6, but Havlicek, Dave Cowens, and Jo Jo White ran away from the Bucks in Game 7, 102-87.

1976 • A second title in three seasons, again led by Havlicek, Cowens, and White, was achieved with a trio of 4-2 playoff series wins, highlighted by what some consider the best game ever: a triple-overtime victory over the Phoenix Suns in Game 5 of the Finals. Three Boston starters fouled out, and unheralded Glenn

McDonald provided 8 critical points in OT as the Celtics won, 128-126. They wrapped up title No. 13 two days later in Phoenix.

1981 • Larry Bird arrived in 1979 and presided over a 32-game improvement in his rookie season, the team's biggest turnaround until the 2008 squad improved by 42 games. In his second season, Bird bagged a title. The Celtics rallied from a 3-1 deficit to beat the 76ers and Julius Erving in the Eastern finals. They won the last three games of the series by a total of 5 points, then dispatched Houston in six games in the Finals.

1984 • In Boston's first of four straight NBA Finals appearances, Gerald Henderson stole the ball and helped the Celtics snag the title. Boston was in danger of losing the first two games at home before Henderson picked off an inbounds pass and sent Game 2 into OT. Boston won, added another OT win in LA, and finally clinched the title with a 111-102 victory in Game 7. Bird averaged 27 points and 14 rebounds in the Finals.

1986 • Bird won his third straight MVP as the Celtics went 67-15 and rolled through the playoffs for title No. 16. Boston swept the Bulls and Michael Jordan, 3-0, beat Atlanta, 4-1, and swept Milwaukee, 4-0, to get to the Finals, where they polished off Houston, upset winners over the Lakers in the West, in six games. It was the third and final title for Boston's Big Three frontcourt of Bird, Kevin McHale, and Robert Parish.

1976
Dave Cowens (18) and Havlicek battle Phoenix's Dick Van Arsdale.

1976 Glenn McDonald (30) shines in the triple-OT thriller.

1984
M.L. Carr celebrates the 7-game victory over the Lakers.

1981
Julius
Erving (6)
swoops in
too late
to defend
Larry Bird.

Bird battles the Bulls' John Paxson.

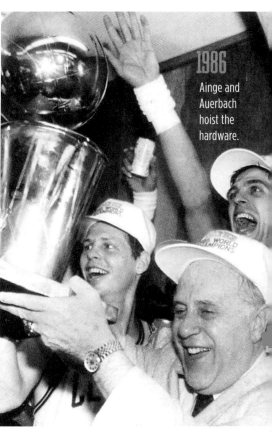

1986

Ainge and Auerbach hoist the hardware.

1986

Ainge, Bird, Johnson, McHale, and Parish – five guys, 67 wins, title No. 16.

SHAPING THE NEW CELTICS

Even before the final ping-pong ball dropped at the NBA draft lottery in May 2007, Celtics co-owner Wyc Grousbeck knew the numbers weren't going the team's way. The two top picks were out of reach, and with them perhaps his dream of restoring the luster of the Green anytime soon.

"Going through my mind after the lottery," said Grousbeck, "was 'How are we going to do it now?'"

What a difference a miracle year makes.

Out of that crushing lottery loss came, paradoxically, the freedom to go another way. General manager Danny Ainge (pictured at right) quickly dealt the No. 5 pick, along with two other players, for Seattle star Ray Allen. The arrival of Allen would make the coming of Kevin Garnett, also known as the Big Ticket, a stunning reality.

The turnaround has exceeded Grousbeck's wildest imaginings. The team won 66 games — the biggest one-season turnaround in NBA history — and turned into a box-office smash. The Celtics filled the TD Banknorth Garden for all 41 home games, compared with nine sellouts in 2006-07, and also became the NBA's top road draw.

For his efforts, Ainge was named The Sporting News NBA Executive of the Year. The only other Celtics executive to win the award since it was first awarded in 1973 was Red Auerbach in 1980.

"The key to putting this team in place, like I've always said, starts with ownership," Ainge said. "And the owners have done some good things to make all of us look good."

Besides Garnett and Allen, Ainge picked up rookie Glen Davis via trade and signed free agents James Posey, P.J. Brown, Sam Cassell, and Eddie House.

"This ownership group went all in," said NBA commissioner David Stern, noting that the Celtics didn't just go after established stars but also costly veterans to fill out the bench. "When owners sense a real opportunity, they do transformational things, knowing the riskiest part is that there can only be one champion."

The owners have never been shy about their ambitions. When the initial ownership group of Grousbeck (above right), his father, Irv, and Steve Pagliuca (above left) committed to purchase the Celtics for $360 million in September 2002, they operated under the company name "Game 7, LLC."

And after they took control in December of that year, the company name that has appeared on the players' paychecks is "Banner 17," a reminder of where their priorities lie. But the team the Grousbecks and Pagliuca inherited was far from championship caliber. Not enough talent. Not enough emphasis on player development. Not enough tradeable assets. The owners and Ainge set about to change that.

It took five years of watching young players alternately shine and stumble, a stream of trades and transactions orchestrated by Ainge, and the stamina to survive a 24-win season last year — including a franchise-record 18-game losing streak — to get to this point.

As the Celtics' success this season reminded fans of previous championship years, the team became an increasingly attractive investment. According to Grousbeck, a buyer recently offered $600 million for the team, but it is not for sale. The current ownership is looking at a tenure that stretches 20 years and beyond.

• SHIRA SPRINGER AND MARC J. SPEARS/ *Globe Staff*

"The key to putting this team in place starts with ownership."

DOC

Derek Fisher of the Los Angeles Lakers summed it up perfectly when he called this Celtics team "the perfect storm." But it wasn't just the presence of three title-starved, veteran players all pointing to one common goal. As much as Kevin Garnett, Ray Allen, and Paul Pierce wanted to get that elusive first championship, their collective desire in no way surpassed that of their coach, Glenn "Doc" Rivers.

"He never won it as a player, so this has got to be a big thing for him," Fisher said.

Think about it: As a player, Rivers never played in an NBA Finals (although his team did). He looks back now and sees three NBA titles that slipped through his hands. As a coach, he'd never even won a playoff series before 2008.

"When he was a player, he had longevity," said Rivers's agent and longtime pal, Lonnie Cooper. "I think he had an empty feeling when he retired that he never played for a champion."

Rivers's Atlanta Hawks teams in the 1980s were good, just not good enough. They never could get by Boston or Detroit or Chicago.

"In that time, we believed we had a chance, we really did," said Randy Wittman, Rivers's backcourt mate in Atlanta and now the coach of the Minnesota Timberwolves. "But we just couldn't get over the hump."

After leaving Atlanta, Rivers came close to getting a ring. In 1993, he played 77 games for the New York Knicks, who had the best record in the Eastern Conference. But that team went down in the conference finals to the eventual champion Chicago Bulls.

In 1994, the Knicks went to the Finals, but Rivers was injured and did not participate in the postseason. The Knicks lost to Houston in seven.

In December of 1994, the Knicks waived Rivers and the Spurs claimed him. He finished the season with San Antonio, which had the best record in the league. The Spurs lost to the eventual champion Rockets in the conference finals.

"I thought we were going to win it that year, I really did," Rivers said. "And when you decide that you're going to win, and it doesn't happen, then it leaves an empty feeling. It has to."

There were tough years in Orlando in his first coaching gig, marked by an unsuccessful courtship of Tim Duncan and a devastating series of injuries to Grant Hill. His Orlando teams made the playoffs but unfailingly lost in the first round. That trend continued in Boston, where his first year ended in another opening-round exit from the postseason.

Rivers will tell you that after many volatile months he in no way envisioned he'd be coaching the team he's coaching.

"I didn't see any of this happening," he said. "Then, all of a sudden, it changes so quickly and you can't help but be excited."

"When I talked to Danny [Ainge] about this job, I said, 'Look, I know we're going young and we're going to struggle, but tell me we are in this thing to win.'"

They were. And they have.

• PETER MAY/*Globe Staff*

RIVERS

"I didn't see any of this happening."

KEVIN

Kevin Garnett always has been The Different One. Innovation is the reason he has a career at all, and he has built a great career in large part because he has kept faith in the same innovation that created the career in the first place. He was the first player in 20 years to enter the National Basketball Association directly out of high school, bypassing the lucrative festival of corruption that is the major college game. People around the NBA wanted him to fail so resoundingly that nobody else would dare try it. People around college basketball wanted him to fail so as to be less of a threat to their pool of cheap labor. He beat them all. He was an all-star by his second season with the Minnesota Timberwolves.

He was a 6-11, 220-pound player who didn't want to play center. He wanted to play facing the basket, slashing past slower, bigger players for thundering dunks, or shooting flossy jump shots over them, and he managed to do that and still average almost 11 1/2 rebounds per game while developing a reputation as the kind of formidable defender that old-school centers were supposed to be. He refashioned his career in such a way as to change the way careers are made. Having done so, he refashioned his position in such a way as to change the way big men play the game. And, having done that, he refashioned the modern idea of the NBA superstar.

He was "KG," or, less artfully, "The Big Ticket," but he was nobody's easy Bling-a-palooza prototype. There always was something Southern and reserved about him — an innate maturity that he used first to confound those people who'd thought he was too young to come into the league when he did. In all things, Kevin Garnett has confounded tradition. He's been the exception that refutes the rule.

Even the way Garnett came to the Celtics was different. When the notion was first bruited about, he was outspoken in his disapproval of the deal. When the five-for-one swap was finally consummated, Garnett was on a

GARNETT
He refashioned the modern idea of the NBA superstar.

cruise. He would come here in his own good time. Since then, along with Ray Allen, who joined the Celtics earlier in the Summer of the Mercenaries, Garnett has revitalized the moribund franchise. By his very presence, he makes Allen even more of a shooting threat and amplifies Paul Pierce's ability to slash to the basket.

Because he confounds tradition, Garnett is deeply rooted in the deepest Celtics tradition of all — innovation itself. They were the first NBA team to integrate. The first to hire a black head coach. They always took chances on players who didn't fit any mold. Nobody in the NBA wanted Bob Cousy because he was a "showboat" who passed behind his back. The Celtics took him. Nobody wanted Bill Russell because he was a 6-9 center who couldn't shoot. The Celtics took him, and they won 11 NBA titles in the next 13 years. The league passed on Dave Cowens because, like Garnett, he was a center who didn't play like one. The Celtics took him and won two more championships.

Larry Bird was slow and white. Kevin McHale was clumsy. Robert Parish was an underachiever, and Dennis Johnson was a malcontent. The Celtics took them all, and they helped bring the entire NBA back from the dead. Kevin Garnett is of a piece with that history. In that, he's not so different at all.

• CHARLES P. PIERCE/*Globe Staff*

PAUL

If Celtics forward Kevin Garnett had presided over the vote, the 2008 NBA MVP award would have gone to his teammate, Paul Pierce, instead of to Los Angeles Lakers star Kobe Bryant.

"I got Paul for MVP this year," Garnett declared in March. "He does a lot of things, just little small things that people don't see. There are only three people I like to watch on offense, and he's one of them, man. He makes scoring look easy. He has an uncanny confidence about him that I love; cockiness and self-assurance.

"There is a reason why I came here," continued Garnett, who won the award himself four years ago with Minnesota. "He's one of the reasons."

On a team with three All-Stars and lots of scoring, Pierce averaged a team-best 19.6 points. He shot 46 percent from the field, a career-best 84.3 percent from the line, and his 3-point percentage of 39.2 was his best since the 2001-02 season. He averaged 5.1 rebounds, 4.5 assists, and 1.3 steals.

"This is probably one of my better seasons overall," said the 10-year veteran.

After the Celtics acquired Garnett and sharpshooter Ray Allen last offseason, a big question was how Pierce would adapt to playing with two fellow perennial All-Stars. The transition has been smooth from the beginning for Pierce, who has maintained his ability to be a dangerous scorer within the framework of the redesigned offense.

"I don't know if I've really adjusted my game," Pierce said. "Shoot, this is the way I've wanted to play if we had players around me. I was a victim of young teams, lesser-talented teams, so I had to do more.

"I know what I'm capable of, a more well-rounded game. I can play at a different pace, know when to turn it up, when not to, because of the guys they have around me."

Pierce's play even prompted an NBA coach to call Doc Rivers to express his admiration.

"He's just been solid," Rivers said. "I'm not going to tell you the coach. But I got a call from a coach, who is a very good coach in our league, one of the best. All he talked about was Paul Pierce and how he changed his game in front of everybody's eyes by doing everything, all the little things: playing defense, being a passer, being a great teammate, just everything.

"For me to hear that from someone else was special. That was nice. He's been that — he's been great."

A year ago, Pierce was upset and confused about the direction of the Celtics, who finished with only 24 wins. He begged executive director of basketball operations Danny Ainge to get him some help and wondered if he would be traded. Ainge more than lived up to his end of the bargain by adding Garnett, Allen, James Posey, Eddie House, Sam Cassell, P.J. Brown, and Glen Davis this season. Considering the struggles of just a year ago, Pierce appreciates everything that is happening.

"I appreciate every moment I get to be around these guys," Pierce said. "When I look back, I don't want to say I didn't take advantage of the guys around me. Each and every day I try to enjoy it."

• MARC J. SPEARS/*Globe Staff*

PIERCE
"I know what
I'm capable of."

RAY

The routine is paramount. People don't understand that. They see Ray Allen, his head meticulously shaved, his jersey tucked carefully into his shorts, his socks pulled up to precisely the same length, and they are drawn to his silky jumper. Can you blame them? It is so smooth, so fluid, so seemingly effortless.

Everyone wants to shoot like Allen. They tell him that all the time. They are envious, they say, of his God-given talent.

"An insult," he says. "God could care less whether I can shoot a jump shot."

Allen leaves nothing to chance. His pregame ritual does not waver: a 90-minute nap, a meal of chicken and white rice, an early arrival time at the gym to stretch. He shaves his head, then walks out to the court, where he methodically takes shots from both baselines, both elbows, and the top of the key.

He is second all-time in 3-pointers, more than 400 shy of Reggie Miller. He has a chance of surpassing Miller, but if he does, it will not be by divine intervention. It will be the result of years of painstaking preparation.

It will also be the byproduct of learning to strike a delicate balance between routine and superstition.

As a child "I had a borderline case of OCD [obsessive compulsive disorder]," Allen explains. "I was never diagnosed, but it was something I was aware of."

When he was 8, he had to drop in five lefty layups and five righty layups before he could leave the gym. Sometimes another team needed the floor and he'd run out of time before he could complete his ritual.

"I cried," the athlete says. "It messed up my day."

He did not discuss his compulsion with his teammates, his coaches, his siblings, or even his mother.

"I was almost embarrassed by it," Allen says. "It was just always beating inside my brain when I was young and trying to make sense of who I was."

They nicknamed him "Hollywood" when he arrived at the University of Connecticut because he was always color-coordinated, always meticulously groomed. He looked like someone important.

"I got that from [Michael] Jordan," Allen says. "When I was a kid, every time he did an interview on television, he was wearing a suit. He looked professional. I told myself, `That's the way to go.'"

The Celtics asked Allen to reinvent himself this season. Now sharing the spotlight with Paul Pierce and Kevin Garnett, he plays fewer minutes, takes fewer shots, and is no longer the focal point of the offense.

The trio of stars has banged into each other and even traded elbows. But, when that happens, Allen has learned to retreat to his corner, regroup, and find a way to adapt.

The bubble he calls the Boston Celtics can get cluttered. Very cluttered. But, according to his careful calculations, there is still plenty of space inside for a championship trophy. Or two.

• JACKIE MACMULLAN/*Globe Staff*

ALLEN

They nicknamed him "Hollywood." He looked
like someone important.

RAJON

Seven years ago, NBA veteran Mike Bibby began mentoring and working out a gangly kid from Kentucky he thought had the potential to play in the league. The Atlanta Hawks point guard definitely has an eye for talent, as that kid, Rajon Rondo, not only made the NBA, he made his playoff debut against Bibby and Atlanta in 2008, as a member of the Boston Celtics.

"You never know what the league is looking for and what the league wants," Bibby said. "But looking at him, I figured he could make it. It's not up to me, but I knew he could be here."

Doug Bibby, Mike Bibby's first cousin, coached Rondo at Louisville Eastern High School his freshman through junior seasons. During Labor Day weekend before Rondo's junior and senior years, Doug Bibby brought Rondo to Sacramento to work out with Mike Bibby, who then starred for the Kings.

"I'm real close to my cousin, and I just talked to him and told him that I was coming out there with this young cat that was special," Doug Bibby said.

Rondo already was being mentored by NBA shooting guard Derek Anderson, a Louisville native now with the Bobcats. But in Mike Bibby, Rondo learned from a fellow point guard. The two backcourt players with the quiet

demeanors spent time together on and off the court. Rondo also worked out with then-Kings guards Bobby Jackson and Mateen Cleaves in Sacramento thanks to Mike Bibby.

"I just tried to help him," Mike Bibby said. "I played one-on-one with him and stuff. I told him that a jump shot in this league was very, very important. I had him working on his shot. I had him working on everything when he came down with my cousin.

"I liked him. He was long, strong, quick. He had it. I was just telling him that you've got to work on your game, that's it."

Rondo said what impressed him most about Mike Bibby during those workouts was his sweet jumper and strong work ethic.

"Mike told me, 'Work hard. Hard work pays off. Stay in the gym even if it's too late or you're tired. Keep pushing yourself. Continue to work hard,'" Rondo said.

With the way Rondo is playing and the experienced backups he has in Sam Cassell and Eddie House, Mike Bibby believes his former pupil is definitely on the right track.

"He's going to be all right," Bibby said. "It's good that he has people around him to help him out. He has Sam now, he has Eddie just to show him the ropes and stuff. It should be easy for him with the guys he has around him. I'm happy for him."
• MARC J. SPEARS/*Globe Staff*

RONDO

"I liked him. He was long, strong, quick. He had it."

RAY ALLEN					TONY ALLEN					P.J. BROWN					SAM CASSELL					GLEN DAVIS				
Connecticut					Oklahoma State					Louisiana Tech					Florida State					Louisiana State				
POS	HT	WT	DOB	YR	POS	HT	WT	DOB	YR	POS	HT	WT	DOB	YR	POS	HT	WT	DOB	YR	POS	HT	WT	DOB	YR
G	6-5	205	07-20-1975	11	G	6-4	213	01-11-1982	3	F-C	6-11	239	10-14-1969	14	G	6-3	185	11-18-1969	14	F	6-9	289	01-01-1986	R

KEVIN GARNETT					EDDIE HOUSE					KENDRICK PERKINS					PAUL PIERCE					SCOT POLLARD				
Farragut Academy HS (Ill.)					Arizona State					Clifton J. Ozen HS (Texas)					Kansas					Kansas				
POS	HT	WT	DOB	YR	POS	HT	WT	DOB	YR	POS	HT	WT	DOB	YR	POS	HT	WT	DOB	YR	POS	HT	WT	DOB	YR
F	6-11	220	05-19-1976	12	G	6-1	175	05-14-1978	7	C	6-10	264	11-10-1984	4	F	6-7	235	10-13-1977	9	C-F	6-11	278	02-12-1975	10

JAMES POSEY					LEON POWE					GABE PRUITT					RAJON RONDO					BRIAN SCALABRINE				
Xavier (Ohio)					California					USC					Kentucky					USC				
POS	HT	WT	DOB	YR	POS	HT	WT	DOB	YR	POS	HT	WT	DOB	YR	POS	HT	WT	DOB	YR	POS	HT	WT	DOB	YR
F	6-8	217	01-13-1977	8	F	6-8	240	01-22-1984	1	G	6-4	170	04-19-1986	R	G	6-1	171	02-22-1986	1	F-C	6-9	235	03-18-1978	6

COACHES

Glenn Rivers was nicknamed "Doc" when he wore a "Dr. J" T-shirt to a basketball camp run by former Marquette coach Rick Majerus. Doc played 13 years in the NBA for four teams before becoming a coach himself.

HEAD COACH

GLENN "DOC" RIVERS
Marquette

ASSISTANT COACHES

ARMOND HILL
Princeton

KEVIN EASTMAN
Richmond

CLIFFORD RAY
Oklahoma

TOM THIBODEAU
Salem State

STRENGTH-AND-CONDITIONING COACHES

BRYAN DOO
Messiah

WALTER NORTON
Boston University

ATHLETIC TRAINER

ED LACERTE
Boston University

DATE	OPPONENT		SCORE	PLACE		NOTABLE
11–2	Washington	W	103-83	2nd	▼ .5	Garnett scored 22 and grabbed 20 in his debut.
11–4	@Toronto	W	98-95 (OT)	1st	▲ .5	Allen (33 pts.) hit winning 3 with 3 seconds left.
11–7	Denver	W	119-93	1st	▲ .5	Celts jumped to 77-38 halftime lead, Pierce had 26.
11–9	Atlanta	W	106-83	1st	▲ .5	Garnett got 27 and 19, with 6 assists and 3 blocks.
11–10	@New Jersey	W	112-101	1st	▲ 1.5	Rivers attended father's funeral, then coached 5th win.
11–13	@Indiana	W	101-86	1st	▲ 2.5	Pierce got 31 and 11, and did pushups between free-throws.
11–14	New Jersey	W	91-69	1st	▲ 3.5	Six Celtics scored in double figures, Garnett had 16.
11–16	Miami	W	92-91	1st	▲ 3.5	Pierce hit game-winning layup with 25 seconds left.
11–18	@Orlando	L	104-102	1st	▲ 3.5	Orlando forced 20 turnovers in Celtics' first loss.
11–21	Golden State	W	105-82	1st	▲ 4	Defense held the Warriors to just 33 percent shooting.
11–23	LA Lakers	W	107-94	1st	▲ 4.5	Perkins scored 21 and grabbed 9 rebounds.
11–24	@Charlotte	W	96-95	1st	▲ 5.5	House steal with 4.7 left set up an Allen 3 for the win.
11–27	@Cleveland	L	109-104 (OT)	1st	▲ 4.5	LeBron James scored 11 of his 38 in overtime.
11–29	NY Knicks	W	104-59	1st	▲ 4.5	Biggest win since 1970, as Big Three sat whole fourth.
11–30	@Miami	W	95-85	1st	▲ 4.5	C's scored 33 points off turnovers, Pierce led with 27.
12–2	Cleveland	W	80-70	1st	▲ 5.5	Celtics' lowest point total in any victory all season.
12–5	@Philadelphia	W	113-103	1st	▲ 6	House and Posey combined to shoot 7-for-13 on 3's.
12–7	Toronto	W	112-84	1st	▲ 7	Celtics moved to 10-0 at home as Garnett scored 23.
12–8	@Chicago	W	92-81	1st	▲ 7.5	Rondo scored 18, Pierce 24, and Garnett 21.
12–12	Sacramento	W	90-78	1st	▲ 6.5	Davis got first career start, scored 16 and grabbed 9.
12–14	Milwaukee	W	104-82	1st	▲ 6.5	C's 12-0 at home, tying best start in team history.
12–16	@Toronto	W	90-77	1st	▲ 7.5	Ninth straight win tied longest streak in 14 years.
12–19	Detroit	L	87-85	1st	▲ 7	Chauncey Billups' 2 free-throws ended perfect home start.
12–21	Chicago	W	107-82	1st	▲ 7.5	Pierce scored 22 and 5 others score in double figures.
12–23	Orlando	W	103-91	1st	▲ 9	Pierce, Garnett, Allen, and Rondo all scored over 20.
12–26	@Sacramento	W	89-69	1st	▲ 9	C's win in Sacramento for the first time in 11 years.
12–27	@Seattle	W	104-96	1st	▲ 10	Pierce scored 37 and Allen got 10 in his Seattle return.
12–29	@Utah	W	104-98	1st	▲ 10.5	C's surpass 2006-2007 win total with 25th victory.
12–30	@LA Lakers	W	110-91	1st	▲ 11	Celtics finish West Coast sweep over LA's short shorts.
1–2	Houston	W	97-93	1st	▲ 11	Garnett scored 26, 11 of them in final 7 minutes.
1–4	Memphis	W	100-96	1st	▲ 12	Tony Allen scored 20 points.
1–5	@Detroit	W	92-85	1st	▲ 12.5	Davis scored 20, the first time a Big 3 didn't lead scorers.
1–9	Charlotte	L	95-83	1st	▲ 12	Jason Richardson's 34 shocked C's at Garden.
1–11	@New Jersey	W	86-77	1st	▲ 12	In 34th game, tied the team record for fastest to 30 wins.
1–12	@Washington	L	85-78	1st	▲ 11.5	Wizards ended game on 15-4 run.
1–14	Washington	L	88-83	1st	▲ 10.5	First back-to-back losses of the year.
1–16	Portland	W	100-90	1st	▲ 11	Allen's 35 were the most he'd score all season.
1–18	Philadelphia	W	116-89	1st	▲ 11	Powe emerged with 10 points in 15 minutes.
1–21	@NY Knicks	W	109-93	1st	▲ 12	Garnett scored 20 with 13 boards.
1–23	Toronto	L	114-112	1st	▲ 11	Raptors hit 15 of 21 three's.
1–25	Minnesota	W	87-86	1st	▲ 11	Garnett steal sealed the game.

DATE	OPPONENT		SCORE	PLACE		NOTABLE
1–27	@Orlando	L	96-93	1st	⬆ 10.5	KG injured, and Hedo Turkoglu hit winning three.
1–29	@Miami	W	117-87	1st	⬆ 11.5	Powe scored 25 and Rondo 23 without KG or Ray Allen.
1–31	Dallas	W	96-90	1st	⬆ 11.5	Pierce and Allen both scored 26.
2–5	@Cleveland	L	114-113	1st	⬆ 11	LeBron had 33 points, 12 assists, and 9 rebounds.
2–6	LA Clippers	W	111-100	1st	⬆ 11.5	Rondo scored 24 to set a career high.
2–8	@Minnesota	W	88-86	1st	⬆ 12.5	Powe hit winning layup as time expired.
2–10	San Antonio	W	98-90	1st	⬆ 12.5	Pierce scored 35 to outduel Tim Duncan's 22.
2–12	@Indiana	W	104-97	1st	⬆ 13.5	Allen had 23 and Pierce had 28.
2–13	NY Knicks	W	111-103	1st	⬆ 13.5	C's head to All-Star break on 5-game winning streak.
2–19	@Denver	L1	124-118	1st	⬆ 13	First loss to Western Conference as KG returned.
2–20	@Golden State	L	119-117	1st	⬆ 12	Baron Davis hit winner with 0.3 left.
2–22	@Phoenix	L	85-77	1st	⬆ 12	Only 3-game losing streak of the year.
2–24	@Portland	W	112-102	1st	⬆ 12	C's recovered from 17-point deficit, Pierce had 30.
2–25	@LA Clippers	W	104-76	1st	⬆ 12	Posey and Pierce led scorers with 17 apiece.
2–27	Cleveland	W	92-87	1st	⬆ 12	C's shot 52 percent, Cavs only 38 percent.
2–29	Charlotte	W	108-100	1st	⬆ 13	Rondo dished out 16 assists.
3–2	Atlanta	W	98-88	1st	⬆ 14	Pierce's 30 made the difference.
3–5	Detroit	W	90-78	1st	⬆ 14.5	Playoff spot clinched as Perkins had 20 rebounds.
3–7	Chicago	W	116-93	1st	⬆ 15.5	P.J. Brown made debut with 3 points.
3–8	@Memphis	W	119-89	1st	⬆ 16	Ray Allen led the way with 23.
3–10	@Philadelphia	W	100-86	1st	⬆ 16.5	C's win 50th for first time since 1991-92.
3–12	Seattle	W	111-82	1st	⬆ 17.5	Tenth straight win led by Allen's 18.
3–14	Utah	L	110-92	1st	⬆ 17.5	Atlantic Division clinched despite loss.
3–15	@Milwaukee	W	99-77	1st	⬆ 18	Cassell got 10 points in first real action with C's.
3–17	@San Antonio	W	93-91	1st	⬆ 19.5	C's overcame 22-point first-half deficit for win.
3–18	@Houston	W	94-74	1st	⬆ 20	Win ended Rockets' 22-game win streak.
3–20	@Dallas	W	94-90	1st	⬆ 20	C's finished season 6-0 against Texas teams.
3–22	@New Orleans	L	113-106	1st	⬆ 20	David West scored 37 for Hornets.
3–24	Philadelphia	L	95-90	1st	⬆ 19.5	Fourth quarter 19-0 run cost C's the game.
3–26	Phoenix	W	117-97	1st	⬆ 19.5	KG got 30 in big win.
3–28	New Orleans	W	112-92	1st	⬆ 20	Pierce led the way with 27 points.
3–30	Miami	W	88-62	1st	⬆ 21	Powe scored 17 and had 13 rebounds.
4–1	@Chicago	W	106-92	1st	⬆ 21	Allen hit 5-of-7 on 3's and Pierce was 4-of-5.
4–2	Indiana	W	92-77	1st	⬆ 22	Garnett had 25th double-double in 60th win.
4–5	@Charlotte	W	101-78	1st	⬆ 22.5	Home court clinched, and best turnaround complete.
4–8	@Milwaukee	W	107-104 (OT)	1st	⬆ 23	Eddie House's 3 made the difference.
4–9	@Washington	L	109-95	1st	⬆ 22	Wizards took third game from C's, most of any team.
4–11	Milwaukee	W	102-86	1st	⬆ 23	Rondo had 16 points and 10 assists.
4–12	@Atlanta	W	99-89	1st	⬆ 23.5	Cassell scored 15 of his 20 in the fourth.
4–14	@NY Knicks	W	99-93	1st	⬆ 24	Big Three all sat, Rondo led in all offensive categories.
4–16	New Jersey	W	105-94	1st	⬆ 25	Powe's career high 27 led the way in finale.

UBUNTU!